To Grevel

With be

EUPHONICS

John Michell

EUPHONICS

A POET'S DICTIONARY OF SOUNDS

COMPILED, WITH AN INTRODUCTION
AND RHYMING ILLUSTRATIONS BY
JOHN MICHELL
AND WITH LINEAR ILLUSTRATIONS BY
MERRILY HARPUR

FRONTIER

First published by
Frontier Publishing
Windetts, Kirstead, Norfolk NR15 1BR

British Library CIP data:
Michell, John
Euphonics: a poet's dictionary of sounds.
1. Spoken language. Sounds. Change
I. Title
414

ISBN 0 9508701 6 1

Illustrations © Merrily Harpur
Design Richard Adams/AdCo Associates
Typesetting Cecilia Boggis/Cecilia Boggis Typesetting, Bedford
Christabel Gurney/Wayzgoose, London.

Printed in Great Britain
By F. Crowe & Sons, Norwich

List of Contents

An Introduction to Euphonics 7
A. A daring aviator aloft in the atmosphere 15
B. Big breasted and broad in the beam 17
C. Cringing in the corner 19
C. Cutting corn with a sickle 21
CH. Cheap and cheerful but itching to scratch 23
D. Down in the dumps or dead as a dodo 25
E. 'Eeeek!' she squealed, 'It's eerie in here' 27
F. Footloose and fancy-free 29
FA. Fanny's failure 31
G. Bogged down in a greasy quagmire 33
H. Hopes of heaven 35
I. A little bit of grit 37
I. I'm a private individual 39
I. The egg and eye 41
J. A jolly jingle 43
K. A quick flick of the whisk 45
L. Lingering by a limpid lagoon 47
M. Warm meals, home comforts and Mother's moods 49
N. Inwardly denying 51
O. OU. Our noble mother 53
P. The pride of the progenitor 55
P. Pompous little pipsqueak 57
Q. Quaint and quizzical 59
R. Running round the rugged rocks 61
S. SCH. SL.. Swine slurping swill 63
SP. Spirit of springtime 65
STR. Strict instructions 67
T. A tintinabulation of tiny, tinny trinkets 69
T. TR. Trouble in store 71
U. Utterly uncouth 73
V. Vital and vigorous but vain and vicious 75
W. Washed away by waves of water 77
X. The box of tricks 79
Y. Yowling yobbos 81
Z. Dazzled by the puzzle of the fizzle 83

An Introduction to Euphonics

Names are important, particularly in public life and when one is young and self-conscious. Actors, politicians and businessmen are prone to worry about such things, and adolescents who suffer under a name they deem ridiculous or inappropriate commonly exchange it for one which better expresses their personality, as they see it.

Personal names acquire historical associations (Winston, Marilyn) and sometimes express moral qualities (Faith, Prudence), which make them more or less popular at different periods. But apart from the flow of fashion, names may be seen as having their own peculiar characters, formed by nothing more substantial than the logic of alliteration. So parents agonize about the right names for their children, whether Polly sounds too pert or Deirdre rather depressing, Bill too blunt, Willie too weak, and whether the alliterative tendency of nicknames might land them with a cheeky Charlie, big Bertha or slippery Sid.

This may seem childish and neurotic, but behind such trivia lies a feature of language which poets have always, more or less consciously, acknowledged. Names and words are made up of sounds, and each sound has some kind of natural meaning, expressing and evoking a certain human emotion. In some cases even the shapes of letters — the serpentine, sibilant S for example — seem to accord with the sounds they denote. Academic linguists and etymologists, amid their serious studies of secular derivations and verbal migrations, have no time for such whimsical notions; but to a poet this aural approach to language is all-important; For the poet — and indeed every sensitive writer — is concerned not only with the proclaimed meaning of words, but also with their esoteric, subliminal qualities, their pitch and ring and the irrational feelings produced by the sound, and sometimes by the sight of them.

Onomatopoeia as defined in the *O.E.D* is, 'Formation of names or words from sounds that resemble those associated with the object or action to be named, or that seem naturally suggestive of its qualities.'

The example given is 'cuckoo', and there are many other words of that description, such as plop, click, buzz, purr, hiss, hem and haw, which are obvious attempts at imitating a sound. Similar attempts are made in all languages. The question which then arises is to what extent these imitative sounds influence the meanings of the longer, composite words in which they occur. This Dictionary is designed to assist its readers' individual judgments on the matter. Its method is to correlate sounds and meanings and, by compilations of words in which certain sounds are dominant, to characterize the effects of those sounds on human sensibilities. Its usefulness will be apparent to poets, dramatists, ritualists, occultists, advertisers, orators and all who require to choose words and sounds for their powers of invocation.

A previous essay on the Poetical Alphabet forms a chapter in a book called *Pluriverse* by the idiosyncratic American philosopher, Benjamin Paul Blood (1832-1919). He begins by telling of a discussion he once had as to why an icicle could not fitly be called a tub, nor vica versa. It is in the nature of its name, he concluded, for a tub to be short and stubby whereas an icicle sounds spindly and slim. At the sound of 'icicle' the irrational mind throws up the word 'bicycle', which is also spindly (and often cold), explaining perhaps the popular acceptance of that word to name a pedal-cranked two-wheeler.

Such verbal associations are notorious afflictions on mental patients, and they also haunt the poetic mind. As part of his dangerous game the poet is forced to receive these germs of madness, to make them welcome and find profit in their visitations. He will also cultivate the art (or nervous compulsion) of rhyming, together with its older companion (commonly used in Teutonic and Old English verse), alliteration, where consonance is in the first rather than the last syllables of words. Alliteration and the spontaneous associations of sounds and meanings are brought together to constitute poetic Euphonics. By that word is implied the most subtle and magical of the ancient sacred sciences, to do with the psychological effects of sound, and the use of music and sonorous speech for the spreading of enchantments.

The primary text in Euphonics is Plato's *Cratylus*, a Socratic dialogue about the origins of language and the influence of archetypal sounds on the formation of words. It is subtitled 'On the Correctness of Names'. The debate is between Socrates and two other characters, Cratylus who claims to know the science of nomenclature and what there is in a name which makes it either correct or otherwise, and Hermogenes who denies that there is any science or inherent correctness in naming things. His contention is that "whatever name you choose to give anything is its right name". The third party, Socrates, examines both arguments and comes down on the side of Cratylus.

The dialogue is long, intricate and in parts quite mystifying. In speculating about the original forms and derivations of names, Socrates teases his listeners with outrageous puns and obscure allusions which modern scholars are at a loss to interpret. He claims no special knowledge of the subject and allows that much of what he says may well be nonsense, but offers the view that "a name appears to be a vocal imitation, and a person who imitates something with his voice names that which he imitates". There are good names and bad ones, and a good name is one that contains the "proper letters". Letters are appropriate or not in a name according as they serve to represent, through their sounds, the qualities of whatever is being named. Thus the proper name for a thing is a composition of those sounds which imitate the ideas associated with it.

Near the end of the dialogue (426 C) Socrates reaches the gist of his thesis in speaking about the inherent meanings in individual sounds. The R sound, he says, is made by the tongue at its most agitated and it is therefore expressive of rapid movement. It also, he adds later, stands for hardness. The Greek words containing R with which Socrates illustrates his statement justify modern interest in this subject, for their English translations also feature the letter R. They include *rhein* (to run or stream), *rhoe* (current), *tromos* (trembling), *trechein* (run, rush, hurry, race) and the words for rend, crush and whirl. Among other examples given are the L sound, which has a sleek, gliding motion, and the G which is gummy and glutinous. The passage is regrettably short, and Socrates does not go on to complete the sonic alphabet.

An objection raised by Hermogenes is that quite different words for the same thing are used in both Greek and foreign languages. Socrates replies that many words have become corrupt over the period since they were designed, and no longer contain the appropriate sounds. This leads to the question of who it was that composed words in the first place. Socrates reasons that it must have been someone skilled in the art, having a talent for making verbal imitations of things. He observes that if a number of painters are all asked to paint the same scene or object, each of their pictures will look different from the others. Similarly with the word-artists: each of them will think up a different word or compilation of sounds to represent the same idea. The fact that in the languages of the world the same things are called by many different names, some of which seem more appropriate than others, is due partly to corruption of the original forms and partly to the differing tastes and whims of the artists who composed the words of each language.

The poet who gives names to things, according to Socrates (389 D), "must know how to embody in sounds and syllables the name of each object which is naturally appropriate to it. Surely, if he is to be an authoritative name-giver, he must make up and bestow all his names with his eye fixed on the absolute or ideal name of what he is naming". Thus the Socratic doctrine of ideal patterns or archetypes which generate the apparent forms of creation is here extended to names. The nature of archetypes is not such as allows them to be copied in perfect detail; human craftsmen can aspire merely to reflect some of their aspects. In the same way, Socrates's ideal names are in the transcendental language of the gods, which is beyond human ken or utterance. The most that name-givers can do, therefore, is to contemplate the essential nature of whatever it is they require to name, and express it as far as possible in the sounds of the word by which they decide to call it. Here again is the lesson, repeated throughout the Platonic works, that the best results in all the arts of life, from carpentry to statesmanship, are obtained through study and imitation of abstract ideals.

That style of philosophy, and the mystical sciences that flourish with it, have a natural and traditional appeal to poets — much to the bafflement of their academic commentators. Rationalism spawns few verses; poets are inclined to cut the professors and turn their backs on the eminent likes of Newton, Locke, Marx and Darwin in favour of more congenial company. William Blake inveighed against the 'single vision' of academic theorists and adopted the comprehensive world-view of Plato and Plotinus. As the Blakean scholar, his fellow-poet Kathleen Raine, has pointed out, the 'darling studies' of the poets are commonly those which their learned contemporaries have considered morbid or discredited. Dante acknowledged the influence of Dionysius and Areopagite, Milton that of Hermes Trismegistos, while Spenser, Shelley, Yeats, Coleridge and Wordsworth were among those who found a prime source of inspiration in the mystical theology of the Neoplatonists. The tradition on which they all drew was that which is most firmly rooted in human nature and has, by its long endurance, earned itself the epithet, perennial. Springing to light in the songs of Orpheus and the ancient law-giving bards, channelled through a golden succession of sages, mystics and devout scholars, it forms that invisible stream which has fertilized the noblest works of literature and wells up spontaneously in the mind of a natural poet.

In the spirit of ancient scholarship, this Dictionary is not definitive, authoritative, exclusive or didactic. As one name-giver, says Socrates, will differ from others in the sounds he chooses to make up his verbal imitations, so readers may find other associations than those here attached to the various sounds. For their benefit, to enter amendments, notes and further illustrations, a page is left white opposite every printed page in the Dictionary. Thereon may be recorded, for example, relevant words in foreign languages. A few such have been included, but for the most part the following verbal illustrations are in English, a composite tongue where the adaptation to rich onomatopoetic effect of words from many different sources has clearly been the work of that shrewd, ever-active name-giver, the native genius.

In light and humorous verse the use of alliteration, onomatopoeia and suchlike devices may well be exaggerated, as for example in Hood's "Ben Battle was a soldier bold", where the blustering B is repeated to comic effect. Coarse rhymes and alliterations are also appropriate in the lowest of poetic forms, the warcry or slogan. Thus: Power to the people!, Ban the bomb! and No taxation without representation! In higher forms of the medium poets are inclined not to flaunt such techniques, but rather to evade pedantic analysis by concealing their art. Yet on every level the art of poetry is bound up with Euphonics and the subtle relationships between sound and meaning. The subject of this Dictionary is thus of assured interest to all who in any way practise that art, and the Compiler anticipates the approval of all poets towards his purpose, however inadequate the results. His hopes are for readers' pleasure in the wisdom and humour which lie in the Socratic philosophy of names, or at least that they may derive some amusement and stimulation from these pages.

The Dictionary

So perhaps a man who knows
about names considers their value,
and is not confused if some letter
is added, transposed or subtracted,
or even if the force of the name is
expressed in entirely different
letters

Plato, *Cratylus*

A. A daring aviator aloft in the atmosphere

A. A daring aviator aloft in the atmosphere

A Japanese sage gives the explanation of why people falling off buildings shout Aaaaaa! on their way downwards. It is because they naturally wish to ascend, and the Aaaaaa! sound is characteristic of uplift, whether in body or spirit. A gives a sense of alacrity, of active, happy, alert, agile, attentive, aware, awake lads and lasses. The appropriate bird is the lark, which might thus be addressed:

Audacious avian arise!
Ascend aloft to azure skies!
Alert to your angelic strain
Our aspirations soar again.

B. Big breasted and broad in the beam

B. Big breasted and broad in the beam

The shape of the letter B can be described as double or binary. It is an oval squashed into two bulges, like bi-focal spectacles, and the B sound is predominant in the names, both proper and vulgar, given to the bipartite bulges of the body: bust, bosom, breasts, boobs, bubs, bum, buttocks, butt, base, beam, bottom, backside.

A bull has balls or bollocks, and a beer-bibber grows a big belly (*Bierbauch*) like a tub, barrel or bloated bladder.

An image evoked by the B sound is of balloons blown up near to bursting. They are broad, bluff, burly, obese, bulging, bulbous, burgeoning, billowing, blooming, blubbery blimps. These bouncing orbs attract adjectives of bounty: blessed, benevolent, benign, abundant, bland, buttery.

But bulbous bubbles also have the sound of bumptious bullies, who are: bold, brash, brazen, bothersome, beefy, brawny, bellicose, brutal bigots or bossy bounders, given to brawling, blustering, blundering, squabbling, slobbering, blubbering, biffing, bashing, brow-beating, butting, bumping and boring. Bucolic and flabby, they boom, bawl, bray, bleat and belly-ache, and are boastful, bombastic braggarts, babbling bullshit, blah-blah and balderdash.

The brutal bluster of a blundering buffoon is the type of energy expressed by B.

Big Bill was as broad as a barrel of beer;
At bruising and boozing he hadn't a peer.
A burly club bouncer he drubbed one and all
Until clobbered and bashed in a brutal pub brawl.

C. Cringing in the corner

C. Cringing in the corner

The hard C pertains to the core, *coeur* or *centrum,* the symbolic locus of the goddess or receptive principle in nature. Thus, cloister, sanctuary, cathedral (from Greek, a seat or divine couch), crypt, cradle, cozy cot, castle keep.

These are among many epithets of the mystical centre, gateway to the chthonic realm of the earth spirit, the crucible wherein life is generated. It is close, confined and covered in, and the names of its symbols include, cove, chasm, cavern, oracular cave, cleft, crack, creek, cranny, corridor, crevice, crevasse, recess, nook, chink, cavity, crater, corner, closet, cuddy or cubby-hole, cubicle, cupboard, catacomb, carapace, culvert, conduit.

The common reference of these words is to concealed chambers and channels and thus to *cunnus,* which echoes through European languages, as the Basque *kuna,* the Norse *kunta* and the old English cunt. The Roman goddess, Cunina, was in charge of the *cunabula,* cradle or crib, and she offered care, comfort, concern, contentment, consolation, cover and protection, coddling, cuddling, cosseting, crooning, confiding, kissing, clinging and clasping

Michael Dames in his alluring book, *The Silbury Treasure,* describes a prehistoric shrine of Cunina as generatrix at the spring which gives birth to the river Kennet or Cunnit. Among old words in which the CN sound of the goddess's name is heard are, cunicle, meaning a hole or underground passage, cunette, a drainage channel, cundy, a north-country name for a roofed culvret, and lacuna or cavity; also the word, cunning, as of a canny woman, one with knack and occult knowledge.

The C sound implies a cautious, circumspect approach to the oracular catacomb, as in crawl, creep, cringe, cower. This type of motion is associated with low types, crooks, creeps, craven cowards, cranks, criminals and corrupt occultists.

Kind Cunina's chthonic cavity,
Cavern sacred to depravity,
Succours in its covered nooks
Cowards, creeps and cunning crooks.
Craving sanctuary and care
Outcasts seek protection there.

C. Cutting corn with a sickle

C. Cutting corn with a sickle

An emblem of Ceres, goddess of corn, was the sickle. Many other names for cutting instruments are built round the (usually) hard C, which was associated in the previous entry with certain aspects of the female principle. For instance: cutters, clippers, chopper, scissors, sickle, secateurs, scythe, scimitar, scalpel, and — one to relish — snickersnee.

Related to cleaving, culling or cutting are: scar, snick, cicatrice, score, scotch, scratch, scalp, schism, incision, dissection, curtailment.

A sickle was the instrument with which Kronos mutilated his father, Uranos, and awareness of castration seems to be one of the feelings evoked by the hard C.

It is also present in cutting remarks, which are, scathing, scolding, sceptical, scornful, caustic, sarcastic, scurrilous, acute, acerbic, acid and acrimonious.

Ken is a critic, a scurrilous scold.
His comments are sceptical, acid and cold.
By caustic remarks and discouraging sneers
He's scarred and curtailed many coming careers.

CH. Cheap and cheerful but itching to scratch

CH. Cheap and cheerful but itching to scratch

CH at the beginning of a word gives a chirpy sound, as of cheeky chicks and chappies who cheep, chirp, chaff, chant, chortle, chuckle, exchange chit-chat and are cherished for their cheery charm.

In the last syllable of a word the CH or TCH sound is of an irritating fidget, as in: itch, stitch, scratch, twitch, a hitch, a catch, a tetchy, touchy bitch, wretched kitsch. Its petulant, crochety air is in:

'Richard,' said Brigit, 'Don't
fidget and twitch,
Stop scratching your chin, give
your britches a hitch.
You look such a wretch with that
blotch on your boot
And I'm itching to chuck out that
cheap checkered suit.'

D. Down in the dumps or dead as a dodo

D. Down in the dumps or dead as a dodo

D has the ring of death, doomsday and sad endings. As an initial it implies loss or lessening, demotion, dismissal, diminution, degredation. As a final letter it tells of deeds dead and done. Dread, which has a D at each end, sums it up.

The depressing effect of D may be detected in the following incantation:

dim, dumb, dingy, droop, done down,
dark, dank, drear, disgraceful, drown,
damp, dump, dismal, damned, dire, dread,
drop, dope, doleful, doddering, dead.

Particularly dreary is the DGE sound, as in, dredge, drudge, trudge, dungeon, sludge, smudge, stodgy porridge, curmudgeon, grudge and dudgeon. See also G.

"STAND FOR THE GOSPEL,
SIT FOR THE EPISTLE;
STAND FOR THE PORRIDGE,
SIT FOR THE GRISTLE."
J.

Down in a dungeon dank and
dread,
Dreary despondent, droops my
dismal head.
A dark, depressing death will be
my dire doom,
Abandoned underground, this
dug-out for my tomb.

E. 'Eeeek!' she squealed, 'It's eerie in here.'

E. 'Eeeek!' she squealed, 'It's eerie in here.'

The short E is too common to have individual character, but the long E, drawn out in the cry of eeeee, is a sound of grief, and supernatural terror. It puts a shiver in the words, creepy, weird, eerie, fearsome, feverish dream, evil demon, and it resounds in verbs of distress, such as, keen, weep, shriek, scream, screech, squeak, squeal, plead and beseech. The keening sound uttered by the ominous Irish wraith-woman, the banshee, is heard in the last syllable of her name.

A classic example of the use of the E and other long vowel sounds to brew up a dense, solemn, uncanny atmosphere is in the opening lines of Poe's 'The Raven' ('Once upon a midnight dreary . . .'). The following is a travesty with added eeees.

Once from dreams of mystic
meaning
I awoke to sounds of keening,
Sounds which seemed to echo
from a being with a greenish
gleam.
Flickering o'er its evil features
Scenes of weird demonic creatures
Teased my brain — I could but
scream.
The doctor said, 'You'll be all
right.
Just turn the TV off at night.'

F. Footloose and fancy-free

F. Footloose and fancy-free

F has a frightfully flippant sound, especially in conjunction with L. It seems to imitate a flag unfurled, flapping in the wind. It is applied to flappers of all kinds, from those that fly to those who are flighty, who frolic and flirt with fops and are called flibbertigibbets or footloose and fancy-free.

An image of F is a frivolous flock of fowls, a flight of feathered fools. In fantastic fashion they flash, flail, fan and flutter their flimsy finery, fussed and flustered as they fidget, flit, flounce, drift and float free, flourishing their flim-flam frippery and flaunting fleecy, flossy, frilly taffeta frocks, fringed with ruffles, flaring, flaming, flagrant and flamboyant. Such flippant, fashionable, frothy folk are famous for flair and effervescence.

Frivolous, flighty fairies flutter
by,
Frisk and flirt and flaunt their
frilly stuff,
Flustering the flitting butterfly,
Floating free as feathers, foam or
fluff.

FA. Fanny's failure

FA. Fanny's failure

A sound of fizzling out is sometimes heard in words with F, often when A is also present. In the word, failure, the F which precedes the wailing sound suggests that before the fiasco there was a certain amount of fun, folly or futile effort. The word for a brief flight and a spattering fall is properly expressive — flop!

Fanny fancied flying but her flaps
were false and frail.
She flailed and fluttered feverishly
for fear that she might fail.
Finally she faltered, forced by fits
and faints to stop,
Fell down feeling foolish, a fiasco
and a flop.

G. Bogged down in a greasy quagmire

G. Bogged down in a greasy quagmire

Socrates in *Cratylus* said that when the first inventor of names observed that the slide of the tongue was blocked by the G sound, he made use of that sound to form words such as *glischron* (glutinous), *gluku* (glucose, sweet) and *gloiodes* (gluey). The type of movement indicated by G is a sluggish oozing of disgusting, congealing grease.

The gist or nitty-gritty of a bog, slough or quagmire is: grey-green, greasy, grimy, gloomy, grisly, grim, glum, grievous, gummy, glutinous, gooey, soggy, clogging, plugging, gurgling globs of grunge.

The exclamation of one who falls into it is a hoggish grunt, ugh!

Sounds of GH and KH occur in expressions of disgust and in names of things which provoke them: Yukh! Gross greedy pigs! Filth in Welsh is *achawi*, in French *ca-ca*, and a true note of revulsion is heard in the Yiddish *schmuck*, wherein is another sound of disgust, the SCH.

George and Gert began to slog
Through a grisly, gurgling bog.
"Gosh," gasped George, "What
gummy muck."
"George," gulped Gert, "Good
grief, I'm stuck."

H. Hopes of heaven

H. Hopes of heaven

The aspirate tends to give spiritual uplift to words, even where it is barely heard, as in ghost. Its poetic effect is illustrated by such phrases as: heavenly hosts, ghostly choir, harmony of the spheres, ethereal charm, breath of enchantment, rushing whirlwind, refreshing honesty, heave a sigh, howl by night, high hopes, happy holidays.

Parts of them make up this aspirated, pneumatic, philosophical rhyme:

Holy Pythagoras made his charts
To humanize the heavenly arts.
His highest hope, to charm our
ears
With echoes of the chanting
spheres
Which chime in every heart from
birth
In chorus with the breath of earth.
But no ear hears, no eye can see
The whole ethereal harmony.

I. A little bit of grit

I. A little bit of grit

The sound of the short I expresses light affection or derision. Its diminishing trivializing effect is illustrated in the once popular song which described a yellow polka-dot bikini as 'itsy-bitsy'. The sound T adds extra pettiness.

An infant imp

Shrivelled and skinny is Sid
And Kitty is thin as a kipper,
And Willie their rickety kid
Is a whimpering whisp of a nipper.

He's hideous, wizened and vicious,
Goes rigid or livid or limp,
And Kitty and Sid are suspicious
He was switched for a pixie or
imp.

They took him to Jimmy the
wizard
And Biddy his wife, who said,
"Who
Is this miserable skin of a lizard?
He's the image of Sidney and
you."

I. I’m a private individual

I. I'm a private individual

The letter I is the symbol of the first person, number 1. It is heard in myself, my identity and what I opine, my private ideology. It is also in one's self-image and independent existence as a single individual. In psychoanalysts' parlance the instinctive self is the Id, and an egomaniac is one who makes I into an idol. There is an obvious link between the I and inwardness, prompting associations as: inherent, I'm in here, my inheritance.

Poets who speak in the first person have to be careful with the I sound. It creates a pompous, didactic effect. This effect is exaggerated in the following imitation of a self-important proprietor.

As a private individual I'm not
inclined to mingle.
I prize my independence, I insist
on biding single.
In my isolated island I'm the idol
of my minions
Who identify themselves with my
ideas and my opinions.

I. The egg and eye

I. The egg and eye

The I, the eye and the German *Ei* (egg) are homophones, and each of them has a similar traditional meaning as representing alike the divine I am, whose symbol is a radiant eye, egg or orb, and the individual as microcosm.

The Greek and Latin I is *ego*, a word made up of the egg and its oval or *ovum* shape — egg-O. The I, the eye and the egg thus seem to be ancient companions. Some verbal connections between them are pictured below.

I and O are the sounds which link the solitary self with the totality of things, as in I alone, or I all one. Similarly in German, the word *Alleinsein* (solitude) divides into *all ein sein* (to be all one). Unity is *Einheit* and one's own is *eigen*, wherein occurs the egg sound which is also in *Auge* (eye). See also O.

Ei
Egg

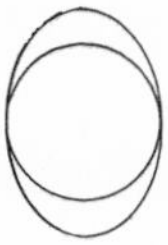

Eye
Auge

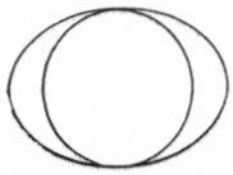

The single visionary eye
Its macrocosm may descry.
At one are those who can atone,
For the All One revolves alone.

J. A jolly jingle

J. A jolly jingle

The pure French J, as in *jeune, joli, jeu, jouet*, seems better adapted to express the jaunty, jingle-jangle associations of the letter than the clogged sound of its English pronounciation, which is as DJ or DGE. That sound at the end of a word has a deadening effect, like sludge (see D), but the initial J imparts a jerky, jittery form of jubilation, as in: a jovial joke, jest or jape, a jag, jamboree, jubilee or junket, jazz, jive, jig, jog, judder and jitterbug, a jabbering jay, jolly Jack, jumping for joy.

These words have an air of somewhat garish jollity, and the harshness of the J sound is heard in jarring jabber and jeering jingles. Its associated colour, *jaune* or orange, becomes sickly in jaundice and jealousy.

A Jubilee jaunt

Jill and Julian Gee enjoyed a joy-
ful jamboree
With a jaunt along the hedges to
rejoice
In the jangling, jarring bray of the
jerky popinjay
And the jewel-hijacking jackdaw's
jeering voice.

When their jubilation faded,
feeling just a trifle jaded,
They adjourned to Jilly's uncle,
Major Plunket.
He's a jovial jackanapes and his
jugglings, jinks and japes
Made a jolly, jokey ending to their
junket.

K. A quick flick of the whisk

K. A quick flick of the whisk

The K sound is a clarion call, like a startled blackbird's ke-ke-ke-ke-ke, commanding attention in: quick! awake! hark! look! prick your ears, perk up.

The words, quick and click, which sound K at both ends, epitomize its function in denoting movements and noises which are brusque, brisk and ephemeral. Its staccato crack is heard after the swishing sound in whisking skirts, and gives a feeling of sparkling spirits in such words as: lark, prank, caper, high jinks, jokey, skipping, skimming, skating, skittish, frisky, kittenish, scamper, scatter-cash, jocular, lucky, cocky, chic, spic and span, cocktail-shaker.

The trivializing effect of K is apparent in: knick-knacks, kick-shaws, bric-a-brac, trinkets, keep-sakes, crackpots, fickle chicks and gimcrack sparklers, tinkling, twinkling and flickering.

Names of small sharp or stinging things tend to be built on the K sound: pick, pike, prickle, spike, beak, stick, crop, cane, icicle, flick-knife. Other cutting instruments are listed under C. With these are administered short, sharp chastisements, generally minor: spank, shake, smack, crack, whack, hack, yank, attack, tweak, jerk, peck, wreck, break, kick, nick, flick, prick, lick, tick-off, tickle, poke, sock, rock, knock.

A false alarm

Quick, Jack! Wake up and act!
Pick up your walking-stick! Look,
we're attacked!
Good luck and be plucky! They're
wicked and slick,
But poking and tickling them may
do the trick.

Alick, you brick, you take the
stick,
Unbuckle your flick-knife and cut
them off quick.
But hark! there's no tinkling of
muskets or tanks.
Despicable trickster! It's one of
your pranks.

L. Lingering by a limpid lagoon

L. Lingering by a limpid lagoon

The L sound expresses light and clarity; its corresponding motion is of languidly gliding liquid, as in a placid, limpid lagoon. Its feeling is leisurely, lazy, flaccid, loose, lax, lounging, laid-back and dilly-dallying.

Preceded by the S sound it becomes slurred, and its character then is slinky and slippery like a slimy slob. Heard in it is a slow, slurping, slithering, slipping, sliding sound as of sleek, slothful slugs. See SL.

Languid lovers lie in Lethe's
valley.
Lethargic, lotus-like, they laze
and dally.
Idly the listless loafers, slaked
with pleasure,
Slump on the lawns, recline and
sleep at leisure.
Stealthy oblivion lulls each sloth-
ful soul.
The swelling floods glide up and
o'er them roll.

M. Warm meals, home comforts and Mother's moods

M. Warm meals, home comforts and Mother's moods

The double-arched shape of the letter M in its mother's eyebrows and breasts is the first pattern to be experienced by an infant, and its first sound is likely to be a murmured, muttered M, which seems a natural symbol of mammals and maternity. Mother is mild, merciful, mollifying and mollicoddling. Her home is humble but warm and comfortable as the womb. Sometimes it is moderately merry and mirthful. Yet home can become monotonous, hum-drum and gloomy, making one morose, miserable, mean, mouldy, melancholy, mournful, moody, mopey, dim, grim and glum.

The association between the cycles of women and the moon that measures the month has caused these words in many different languages to be dominated by the M sound. Under the moon occur mysteries, romances, marvels, miracles, magic and the mantic arts, stimulating imagination or madness and monomania. The M sound evokes images of the dark, mysterious aspect of the female spirit, such as the mystic moon-maiden, the Madonna and the gloomy chasm.

Mother's plump and matronly and
humbly domestic,
Her home is warm and comforting, but modest, not
majestic.
She used to dream of mysteries,
of glamour and romance,
But muddling her money matters
made her miss her chance.

N. Inwardly denying

N. Inwardly denying

The N sound is widely used for negation, as in no, nay, *non, nein, ne, niet*. Socrates identified it as an inward sound, and it does seem appropriate to those who are negative, niggling, introvert, mean and stingy, nagging narrow-minded, nit-picking, snide, sneering, sneaky and nasty. It has an air of denigration which, as Mr Blood observed, "is intensified by drawing up the muscles of contempt at the sides of the nose."

'No, you naughty knave,' nagged
Nurse,
'Nasty sneak! I've known none
worse.
Don't deny you nicked my ring,
Sinful, mean, indecent thing.'

O. OU. Our noble mother

O. OU. Our noble mother

The shape of the letter O is the shape of the mouth producing the round O sound. It is a noble, rolling, resounding, overaweing sound, used to effect in the translation of Homer's invocation to: 'Ocean, the source and origin of the gods'.

O is old, a proto-sound, symbol of the original womb or or the oval world-egg (*ovum, oeuf*). It dominates words meaning either the whole or a hole, totality or void. The whole is the cosmos, world, dome of heaven, globe or orb; a hole is an orifice (*trou*). The womb sound echoes in the names of other round containers: bowl, bower, pot, retort, bottle, oven, and finally the gloomy tomb. Protuberances are also expressed by O, as mound, nob, knob, knoll, blob, bobble, and one who is overblown is pompous, bloated, obese, orotund, roly-poly, obsessed by glory. In some these words the O sound is combined with B to create a blustering effect.

The orb of the moon, the womb of our mother and the rolling downs are poetic phrases typifying the effect of the O sound.

O, goddess of the whole round
globe,
Noble in glorious, glowing robe,
Enthroned beneath a golden
dome,
Your womb our source, come, call
me home.

P. The pride of the progenitor

P. The pride of the progenitor

The sound of the letter P is proud, imperious and priapic. As B suggests the binary bulges of the body and hard C the organs of the female, so P denotes the emblems of paternity, the penis, prick pecker, impregnator, and the letter is shaped accordingly. It proclaims male priority and preeminence and is heard in principalities and powers, emperors and potentates. With reference to the P sound are named things which are perpendicular and rampant, such as piles, poles, posts, props, supports and uprights, pikes, peaks, pales, pinnacles, pillars and pedestals.

A paternal parade

Papa, the President, the principle personage in our Republic, proudly parades his powerful troops past the imperial palace, prinking and preening in peacock plumes and prancing importantly on his prize palfry.

Papa is a prime politician
And proud of his powerful
position.
When people implore his support
for the poor
He spurns and pooh-poohs their
petition.

P. Pompous little pipsqueak

P. Pompous little pipsqueak

When persons become puffed-up, pompous and pretentious they attract the derisory effect of the P sound and are called poor, puny, piffling, piddling, pitiful, petty, pushy, impertinent pups, peanuts, pipsqueaks and poltroons. Another kind of pride makes people prim and proper, prissy, pernickety and precious. They are apt to be contemptuous and pooh-poohing, and their particular exclamation is pshaw! In contrast to the B people who bash and batter, the spiteful P folk pinch, poke pins, prick, pry and prod. Given the same treatment, they turn peevish and pine, pule, puke and complain pathetically.

Pride precedes comeuppance

Proper little popinjay, the population cried
As he pirouetted past them in his panoply of pride.
He preened his purple plumage, posed in postures prim to pert,
Then tripped and sprawled and splattered in a putrid pool of dirt.

Q. Quaint and quizzical

Q. Quaint and quizzical

The Q with its curlicue or curlie *queue* is a funny looking letter, and the odd quirkiness of its appearance seems to extend to its meaning. It sounds in the last syllable of words with a slightly outmoded, whimsical air, such as picturesque, baroque, exquisite, antique, and words to which it provides the initial are quaint, queer, quirky, queasy, quaking and quivering. It is a bit of a fraud in quack doctors, chequered careers and things which are quasi, or not what they seem, and it is quizzical, questioning and querulous in quids and quiddities, qualms and quandaries, quests, quips and quibbles. In Latin languages it queries: *quis? que? quoi? quad? quando?*

A-quiver with zest we embarqued
on a quest
But its quirks made us queer and
uneasy,
Querulous, havering, questioning,
quavering,
Quarrelsome, quibbling and
queasy.

R. Running round the rugged rocks

R. Running round the rugged rocks

The R sound, said Socrates, denotes rapidity and hardness. The first is illustrated by numerous words such as hurry, scurry, rush and tear, run a race, whirr round, revolve, raging torrent roaring current. Hardness and R go together in phrases like: rigid, firm and rugged as a rock of granite. The two qualities are combined in words for abrasive actions such as, break, rend, crush, crumble (given in *Cratylus*), fracture, rupture, grind, rub, crash, scrape and crunch.

Roughly runs the raging torrent
Over rocks and crags abhorrant,
Rolling rapid with a roar
Bursting on the rugged shore.

S. SCH. SL. Swine slurping swill

S. SCH. SL. Swine slurping swill

The sibilant S can be amiable as in whispering and whistling, but it is the hostile hiss of a snake or cat which is heard in spiteful words as, Piss off you stupid ass, stinking skunk! Further disgust is added when the sound is SCH or SL. Combining these with the other common sounds of disgust, G or GH, one arrives at the perfect word for expressing contempt and loathing — schlugh! This ideal was approached by Shakespeare when he named Shylock, and it is rivalled by several Yiddish words of contempt such as *schlock*, *schlepp* and *schmuck*.

Associations of sludge and the slimy serpent (German, *Schlange*) are in words as, slither, slip, slop, slide, slurp, slug, sloth, slur, sly, slouch. In these the gliding, limpid liquid represented by the L sound is sullied by the S, making it a sluggish ooze or slough.

'Since you're such a slippery slug,'
Hissed Sally with a sullen shrug,
'Slink to Susie's sluttish slum.
She's your sort you slimy scum.'

SP. Spirit of springtime

SP. Spirit of springtime

The SP sound of spitting is heard at or near the beginning of many verbs which describe liquid spluttering or splashing out in spate, like sparkling water from a spa or spume splurging from a champagne bottle. They include: spew, spurt, spray, spate, spring, spill, spout, explode, expectorate, expel, spit out.

Spring and spirit are words which sum up the qualities of SP. In all its various meanings spring is to do with jumping up. In springtime sprouts and sprigs spurt ahead and one feels spruce, spry, sprightly, spicy, spic and span, sparky, spunky, spirited, speedy, spontaneous, splendid, inspired, spurred on, ready to sprint at a spanking pace or go on a sporting spree.

A spirited person is either full of aspirations, expectations and *espoir*, or has spasms of spite, spleen and waspishness.

In spring the aspidistras sprout,
Sprightly sprigs and sprays spurt
out.
Spleen is spent; the sparkling air
Dispatches spite, expels despair.

STR. Strict instructions

STR. Strict instructions

The STR sound is strongly connected with straightness and strictness of conduct. Among the names of things which are straight when stretched out are: street, strand, strip, stripe, streak, string. In striding, strutting and straining ahead one naturally goes straight.

Stringency and the striking down of those who ignore strictures or instructions are displayed in the German words, *Strafe* (punishment) and *streng* (stern). Wrong-doers are given strokes of the strap or strop or put under constraint.

A poetic image of the STR sound is a streak of light (German, *Strahl*) streaming or striking straight down a stretch of strand.

The Schoolmaster

My strategy is stern but straight:
Obstructive, strident, obdurate
Striplings who strike or stroll in
late
I strap or treat to strictures.

But those who stringently abide
By my instructions, strict applied,
Who strive ahead with strenuous
stride,
I take them to the pictures.

T. A tintinabulation of tiny, tinny trinkets

T. A tintinabulation of tiny, tinny trinkets

T has a light tinkling sound, stimulating slightly pleasant or irritated feelings, as in the phrases: pretty ditties and tinkling tunes on the spinet; trilling, twittering titmice; titivating chatterers, talkative tell-tales, tittle-tattling over the tea-table; tasty tart, trifle or titbit to tickle, tempt and titillate the appetite.

A trip for two to tea in Tooting gives the general impression.

The type of motion implied by T is dainty and fastidious, tripping, trotting, tip-tapping, tottery. It is the opposite of purposeful and is apt to be called trivial, stupid, futile, pretentious, affected, stuttering, tedious and tiresome. The T sound is applied scornfully to those who are thought to be pretty, trite, tarty, tatty little upstarts, wretches, chits, sluts, twits, gits, twats, twerps and nitwits. When teased, tortured, twitted or tantalized, such people become irritable, testy, tetchy and spiteful and throw fits and temper tantrums.

Tim and Terry take a cottage near
the tiny town of Wittering,
Replete with dainty ornaments
and bits of tinsel glittering.
Through the pretty little patio
you trip onto the terrace
Which its Timmy's task to tidy
when to set the tea is Terry's.

T. TR. Trouble in store

T. TR. Trouble in store

The tremulous sound in T, combined with long vowels and other consonants, particularly R, gives terror to words such as: storm, torrent, trouble, tumult, tornado, tirade, tempest, tantrum and the twisting, twirling *tourbillon* (whirlwind). In high winds and rough seas sailors are tossed, turned, tormented, terrified and made to twitch and tremble.

This town is tormented in terrible forms
By torrents tornadoes and trumpeting storms.
The traders are troubled and tremble afraid
When the thunders intone their tremendous tirade.

U. Utterly uncouth

U. Utterly uncouth

In his essay on the Poetical Alphabet (referred to in our Introduction) Mr Blood amusingly illustrates the blunt, mundane effect of the short U sound:
"U, gutteral, or flat, is a humorous savage, best described in his own words: a huge, lubberly, blundering dunderhead, a blubbering numskull and a dunce, ugly, sullen, dull, clumsy, rugged, gullible, glum, dumpish, lugubrious — a stumbler, mumber, bungler, grumbler, jumbler — a grunter, thumper, tumbler, stunner — a drudge, a trudge; he lugs, tugs, sucks, juggles, and is up to all manner of bulls — a musty, fussy, crusty, disgusting brute, whose head is his mug, his nose is a snub, or a pug, his ears are lugs, his breasts dugs, his bowels guts, his vitals grub, his garments duds, his hat a plug, his child a cub, his dearest diminutive is chub or bub or runt; at his best he is bluff, gruff, blunt; his doublet is of sturdy buff and though not sword, is 'cudgel proof'; budge he will not, but will drub you with a club, or a slug, nub, stub, butt, or rub you with mud — for he is ever in a muss or a fuss — and should you call him grudging curmudgeon he gulps up 'ugh, fudge, stuff, rubbish, humbug' in his dudgeon; he is a rough, a blood-tub, a bummer, and a 'tough cuss' all around; he has some humor, more crudity, but no delicacy; of all nationalities you would take him for a Dutchman."
This inspires an illustrative rhyme:

Doug, the Dutchman in our pub,
Sups a mug and stuffs his grub.
'Ugh!' he gulps and rubs his gut,
Stumbling glumly to his hut.

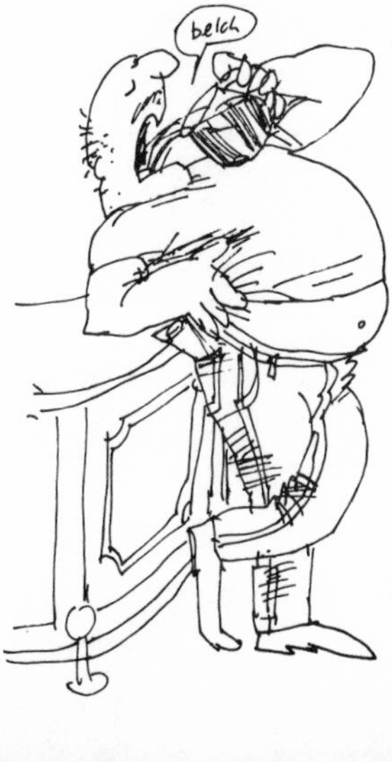

V. Vital and vigorous but vain and vicious

V. Vital and vigorous but vain and vicious

Vitality is in words which relate to the Latin *vita* (life), *vis* (force) and *vigor*. In English are vim and vigour, vitality and velocity. The effect of V can be described as very vivacious.

Like several other sounds the V has a second, opposite meaning. In accordance with its relationship to the sounds W and F, it is sometimes weak and flustered (German, *verwirrt*), as in the words: vain, vacuous, vapid, vague, vacillate, vagrant, vaporous, vertigo, veer and vary. Weakness leads to vice, and so: vile, vicious, depraved, evil, vindictive, violent, virulent, vexacious, vengeful, voracious villain, virago, vermin, viper, vampire, devil. Venomous is best descriptive of the malevolent aspect of V.

Ravished, violently defiled,
Savaged, chivvied, vexed, reviled,
Vows of love I rive and sever.
Vicious vamp! Forgive I'll never.

W. Washed away by waves of water

W. Washed away by waves of water

The shape of the letter W can be described as wavy and watery, and so can the type of motion it implies. In liquids it is an aqueous flow, as in swelling billows. In air it is of whisps of wool or down, wafted away, blown on the winds. Wavering is the state of mind reflected in the W sound; it is weak, wet, weary, weedy, wobbly, wandering, woeful, wistful, willowy, wishy-washy and querulous.

The sense and image of W are depicted in a switchback railway.

A watery walk

When the weather is wet and windy the wells overflow and waves of water wash over the weir. Wearing wellingtons we waddle through the squelchy swamp, wondering which way to wander, whether to wade or swim.

Woes of the wayfarer

Wallowing billows swirl and swell,
Willows wafted swish and sway,
Will-o'-wisps and wraiths do dwell
Down that weird and watery way
Where the wanderer's wavering
howl
Wreathes the wastes in
clouds of woe,
Where the wistful, watchful owl
Waits the hour of dawning glow.

Through that swamp we sweat and
swear,
Wondering which? why? what?
when? where?

X. The box of tricks

X. The box of tricks

The form of the letter X, a cross as of two sticks laid one across the other, depicts a paradox, a meeting of opposites as in sex. Its sound suggests an eccentricity, a box of tricks, by which one is perplexed, vexed, hexed, jinxed, foxed, mixed up and put in a fix. There is a teasing quality to the X sound, as in:

Pixy is a foxy minx,
Full of vexing tricks, a jinx,
Yet she cooks and fixes clocks,
A perplexing paradox!

Y. Yowling yobbos

Y. Yowling yobbos

Y at the end of a word is a sound of familiarity, affectionate or derisive, like the short I. A merry ditty for a pretty baby typifies its associations.

Y as an initial has a coarse, rustic, jeering ring. Curs and rude youths torment with yaps, yelps, yowls, yells, baying and yammering. Makers of such noises are called yobs or yoiks, or yokels meaning rustic clods. Swift's name for human animals in *Gulliver's Travels* was yahoos. People of similar kind in America have been called yippies, and those of another class yuppies. In English novels they yodel yoo-hoo, or yoicks if huntsmen, or yo-ho-ho if piratical.

Yeah! yah! ya-boo! yaroo! are among many expressions of leering mockery based on the Y sound. It is heard in yid, a nasty name for a Jew, also in a nasty epithet for timid folk, yellow. 'You young . . .' followed by some disobliging term, is a style of address traditionally used by irate fathers-in-law.

In German the Y sound is denoted by the letter J and occurs in words of yowling and yelping such as: *jammern, janken* and *jaueln.*

Yowling yobs

Yelping, yapping puppies,
Gangs of jeering kids,
Yelling names at yuppies,
Yokels, Yanks and yids.

Z. Dazzled by the puzzle of the fizzle

Z. Dazzled by the puzzle of the fizzle

There is a line in a half-remembered song which recalls "those lazy, hazy, crazy days of summer". It illustrates the effect of the Z sound in conjuring up the muzzy, fuzzy atmosphere of a hot summer's day, when bees are buzzing, one's eyes are glazed and the mind feels dizzy, dazy, fazed, bemused, woozy and drowsy. From the heads of dozing, snoozing (perhaps boozed) cartoon characters issue the letters zzzzzz.

The Z sound has a quizzical, zealously inquisitive air, apparent in words such as puzzle (which looks a bit like a puzzle), quiz, tease and maze, or miz-maze, which can make one crazy, zany or frenzied. The Z shape recalls the crooked pathway of a maze, also the crooked business wizard, by whom one is swizzled, chizzled and bamboozled. It is the shape of the zig-zag flash of blazing, fizzling, sizzling, dazzling lightning in a blizzard. With this image come the words whizz, zing, zip, zoom and zap.

Impressions given by the Z sound are of a person with zest, trying busily to escape from a maze, or of someone in a tizzy, dazed by a bizarre puzzle and gazing at it in amazement.

Sizzle or doze?

Lizzie's always busy, dizzy,
buzzing round like crazy.
Ebenezer's zonked and sozzled,
dozy, dazed and lazy.
Here's the quiz and puzzle: if
bamboozled and confused
Do you zoom and sizzle or get
hazy and bemused?